Cupid

Valentine's Day Coloring Book

Color Your Heart, Color your Love

Kimberly Hardd

Happy Coloring

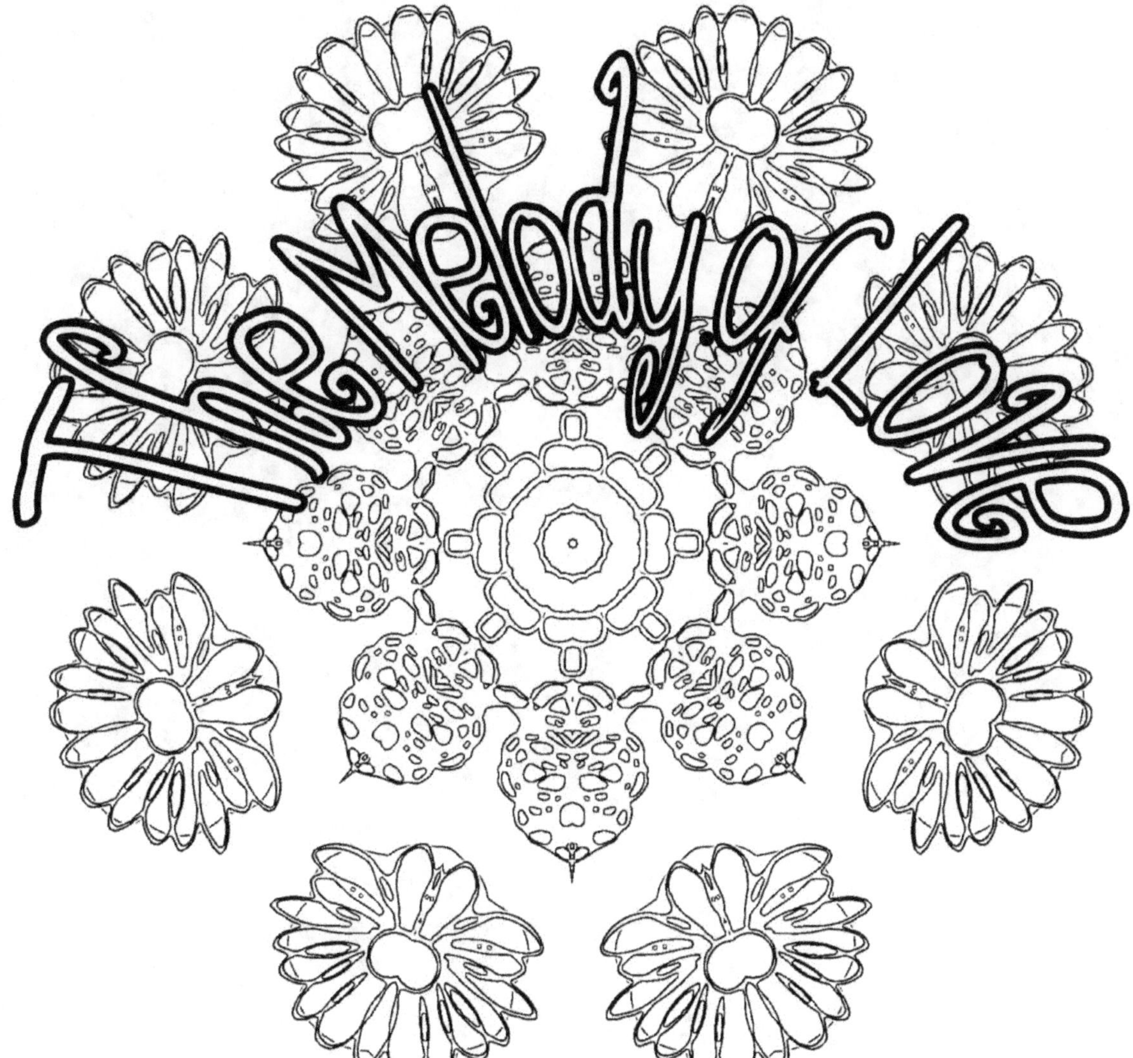
The Melody of Love

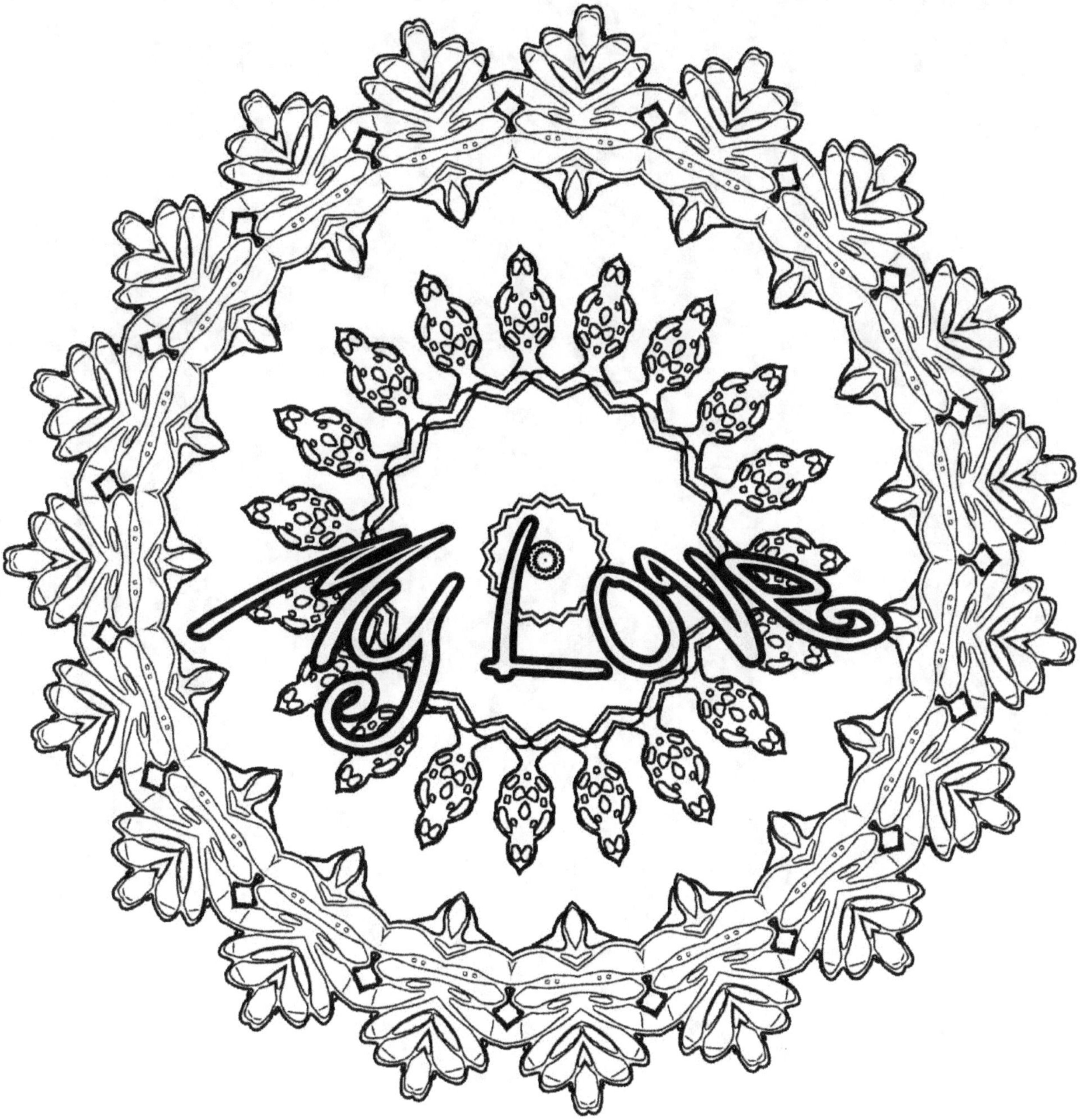
My Love

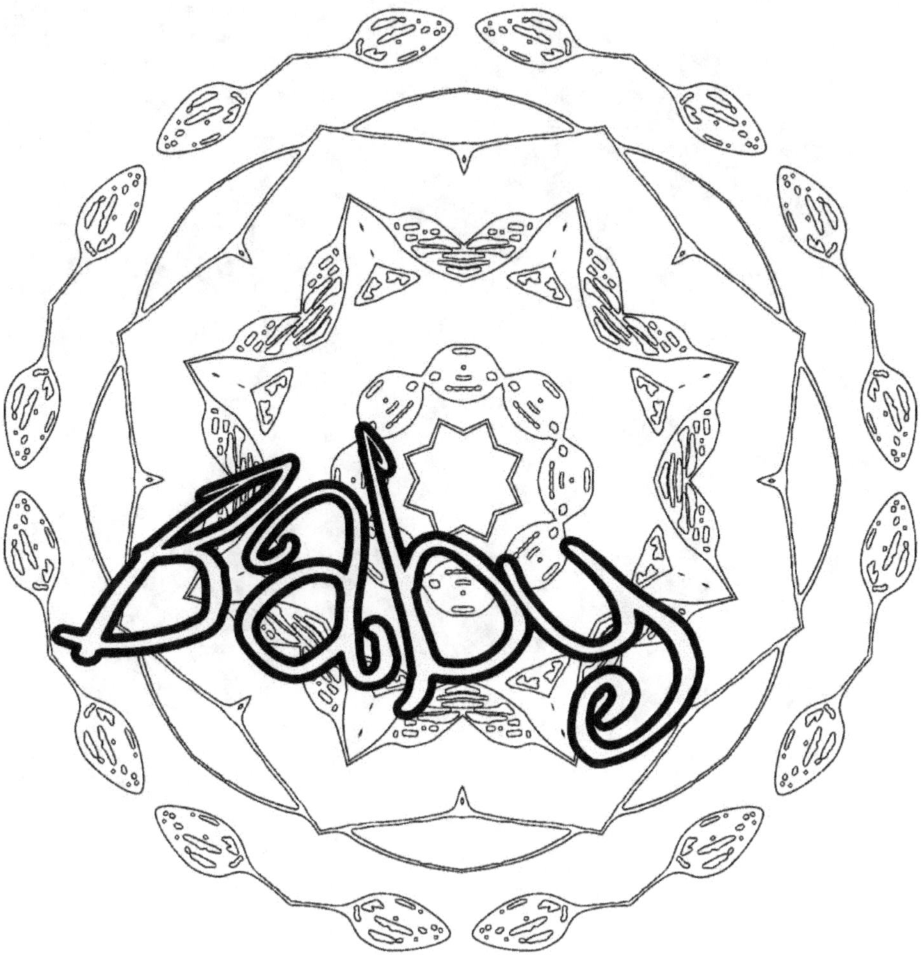
Baby

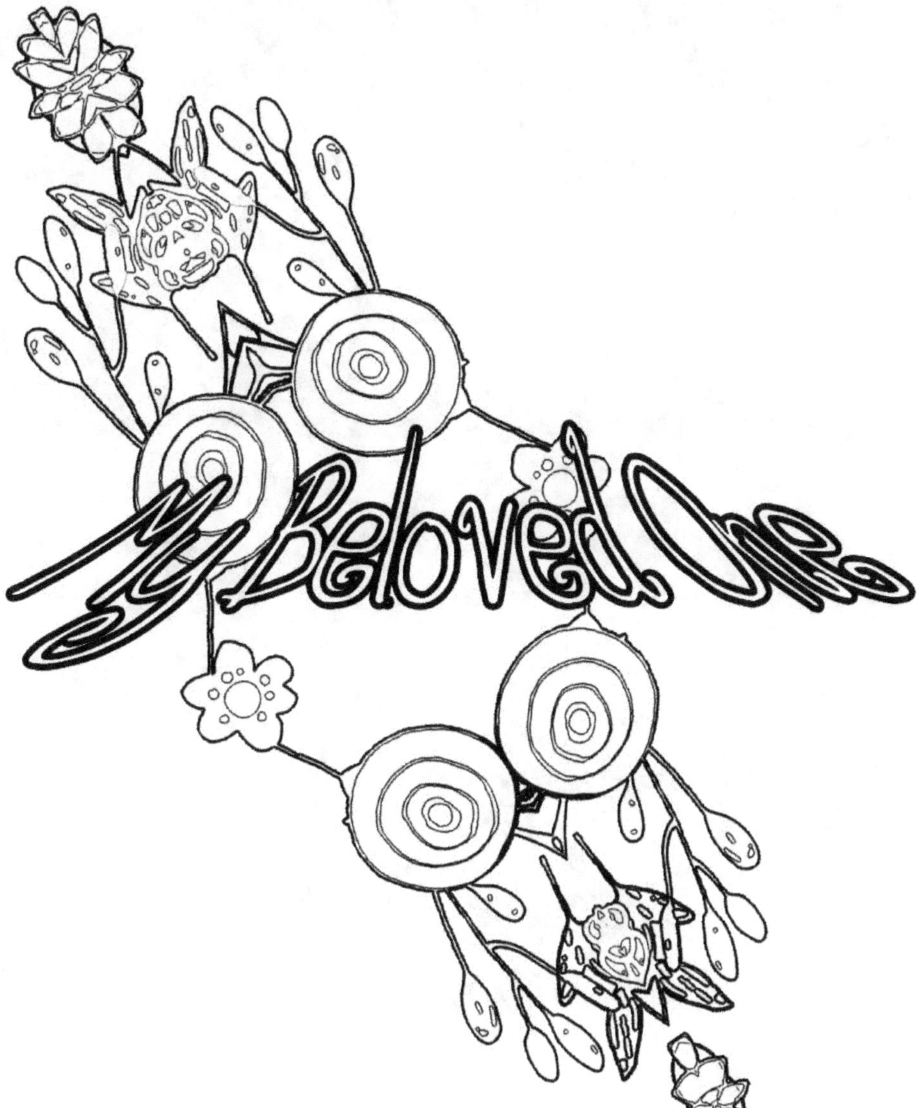
My Beloved One

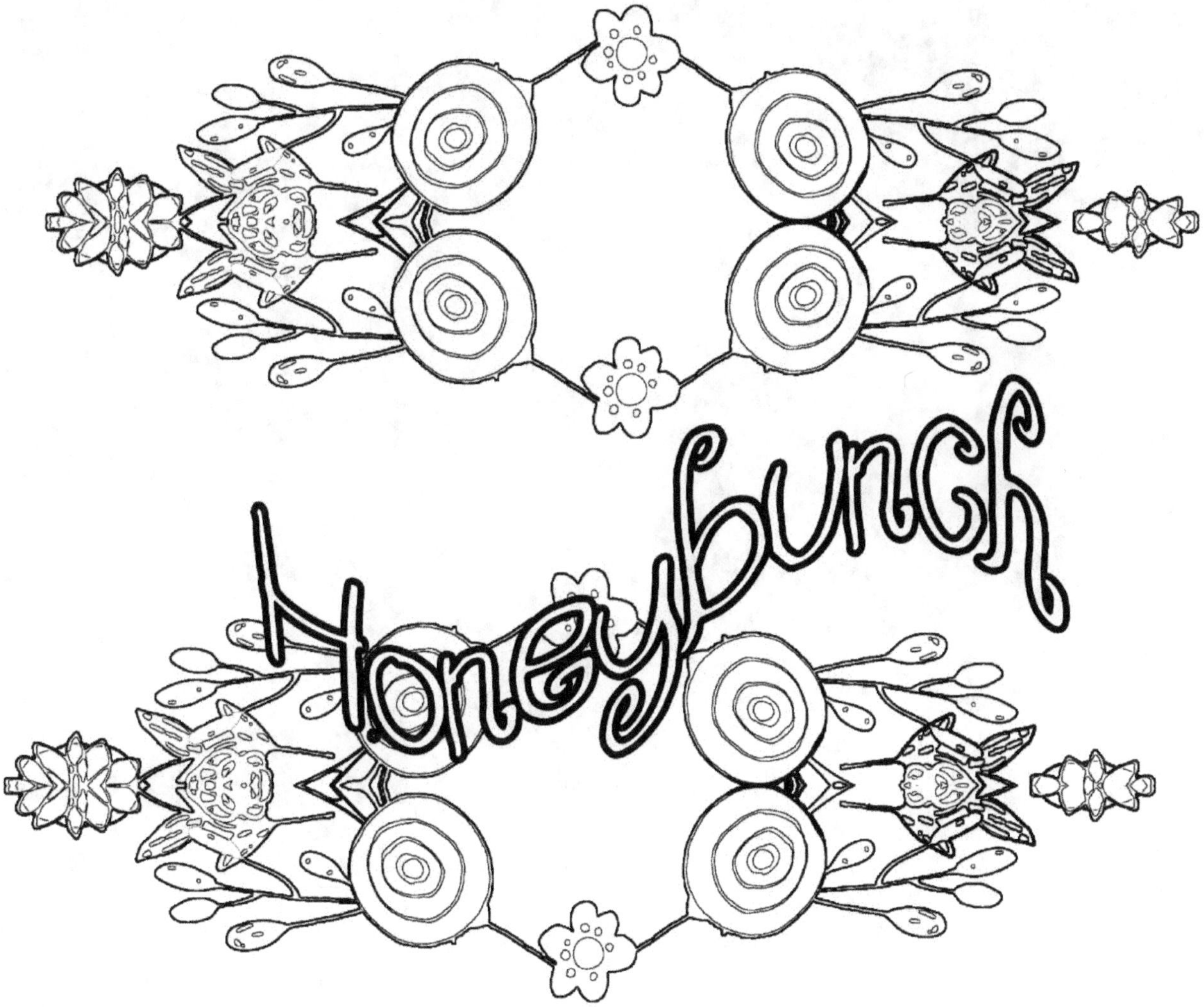
Honeybunch

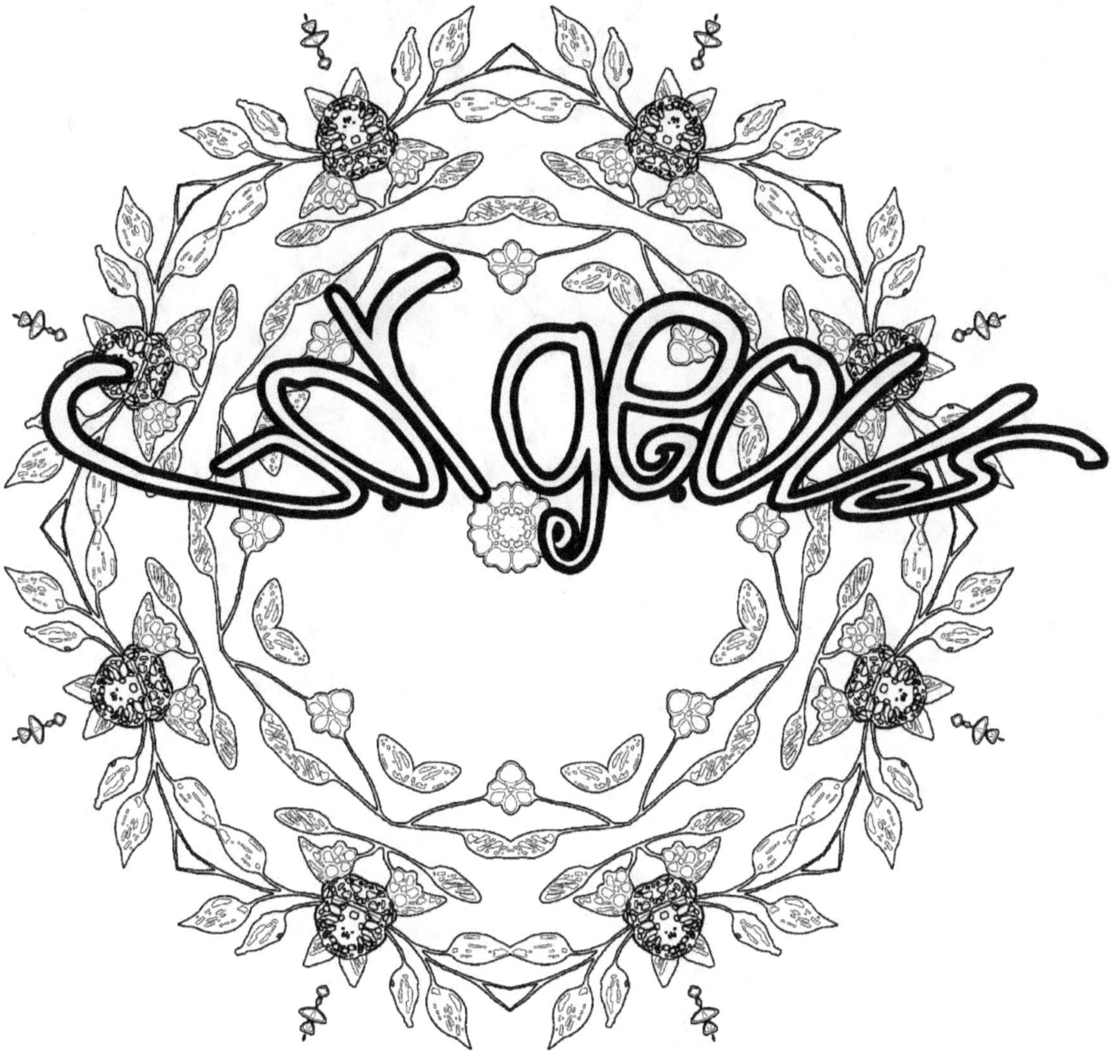

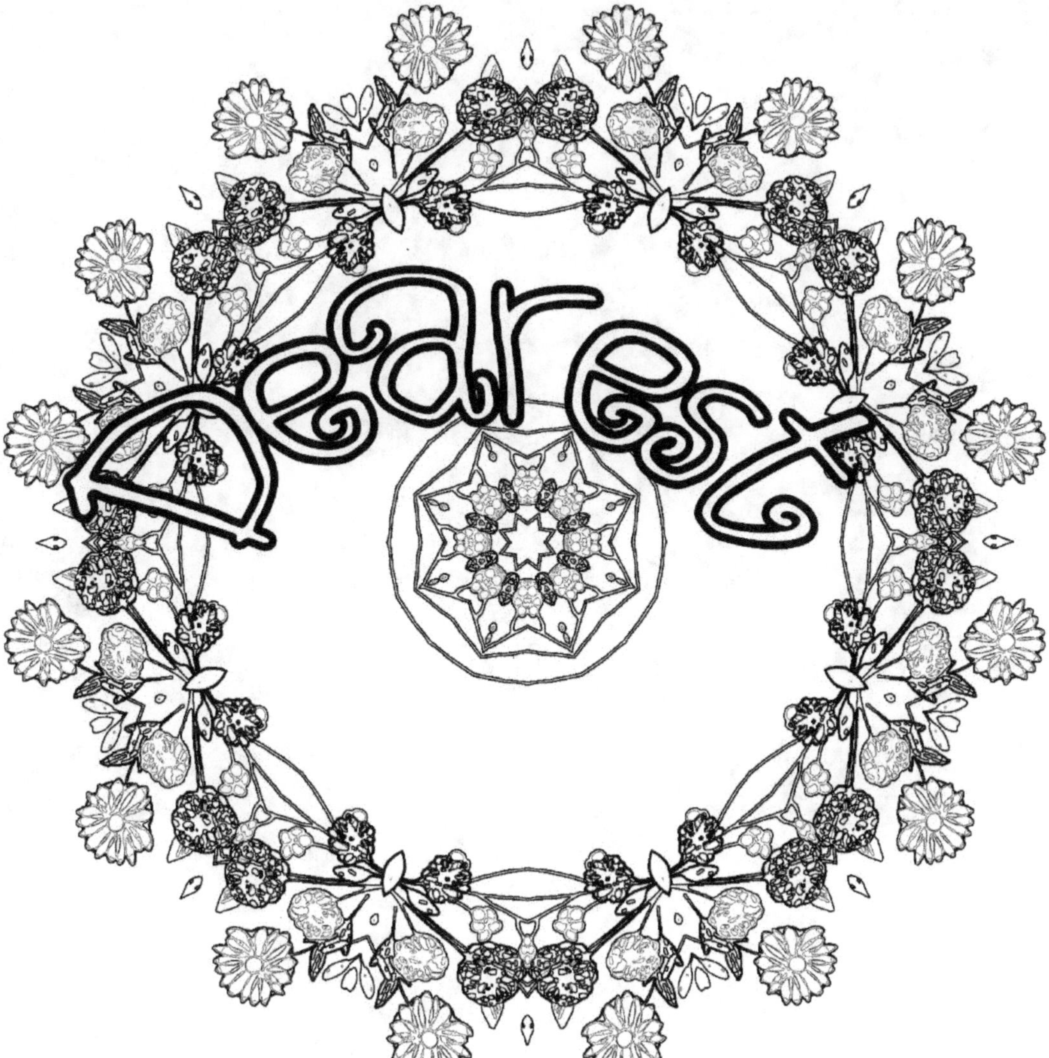
Dearest

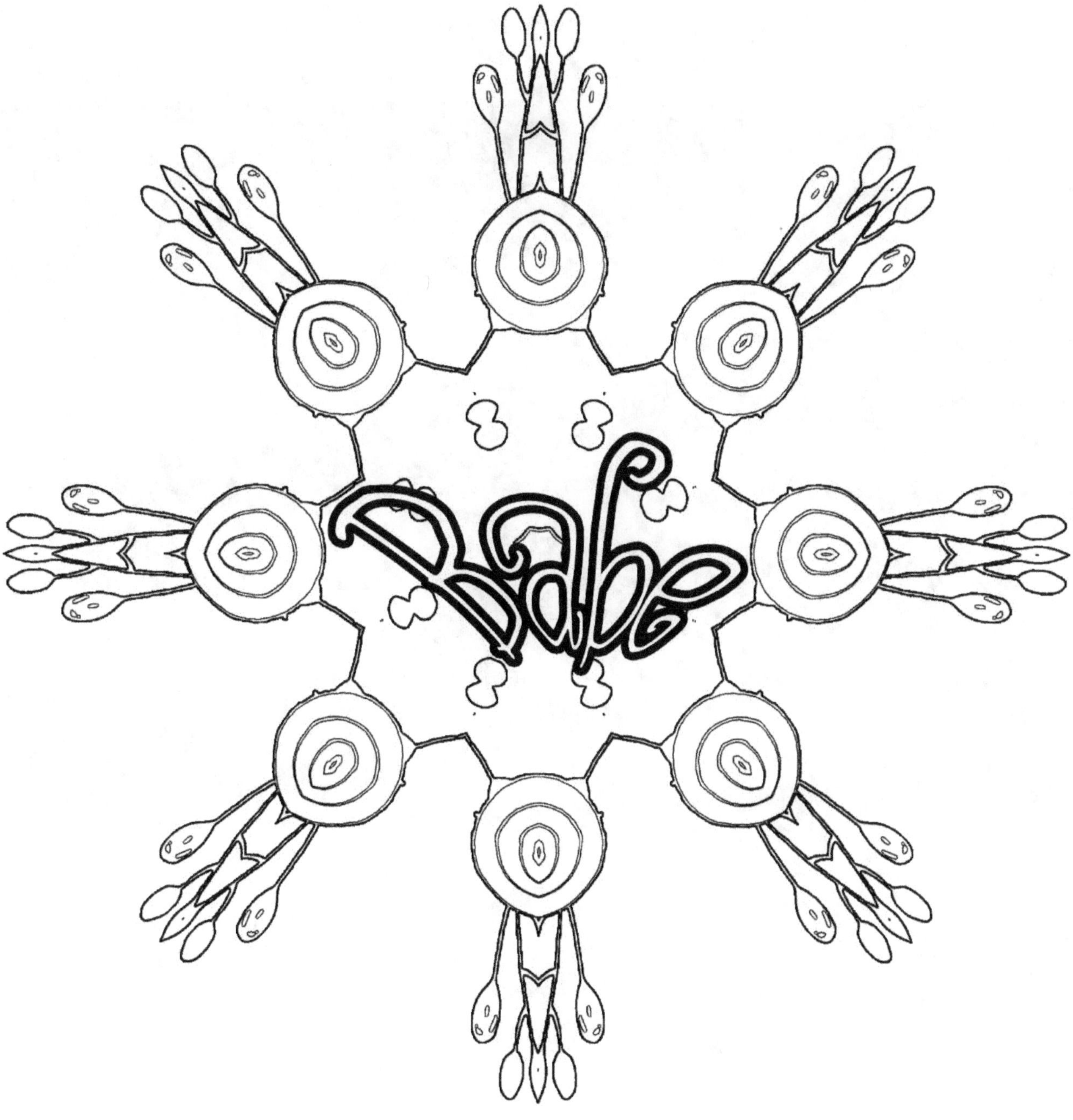
Babe

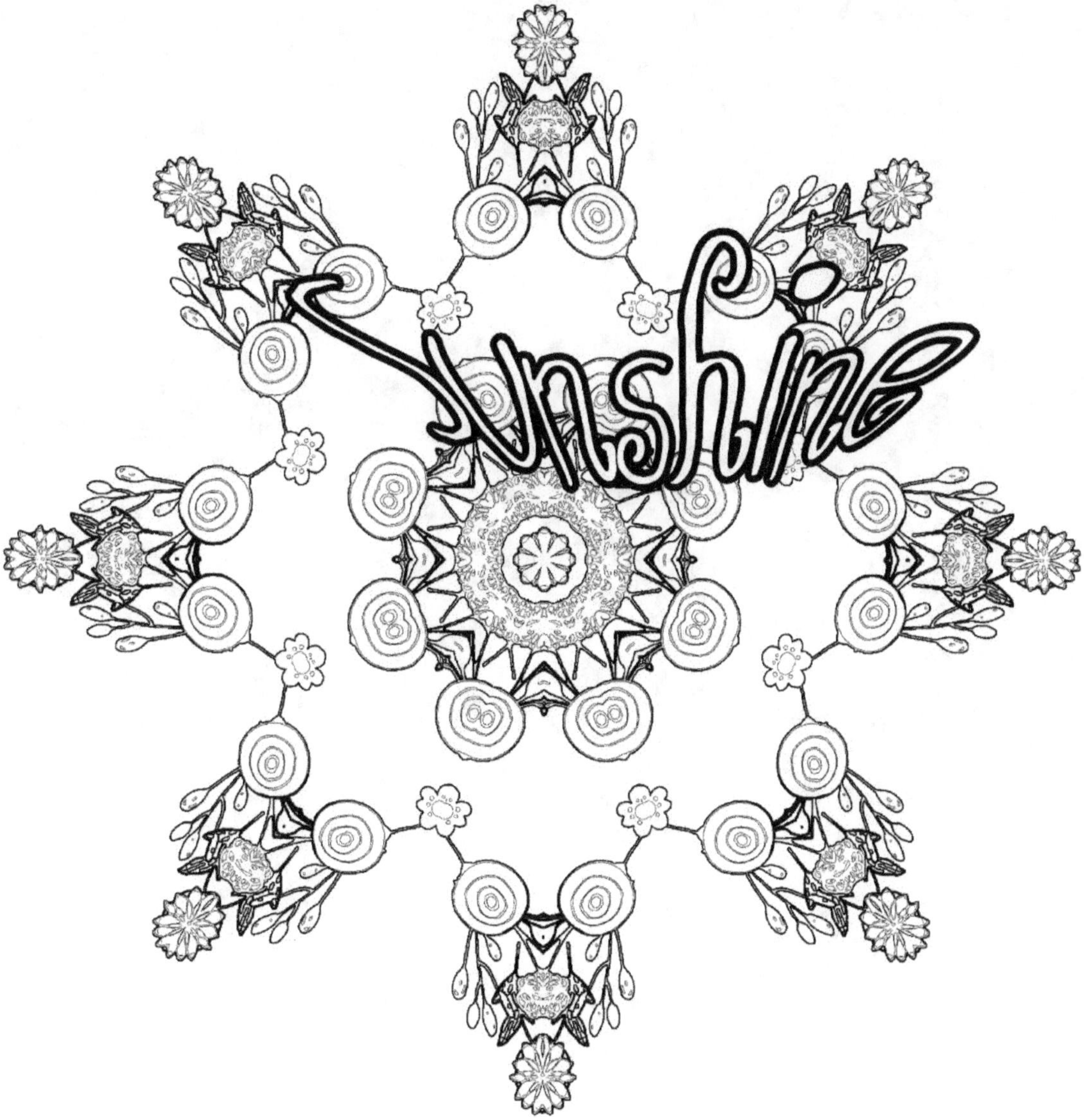
Sunshine

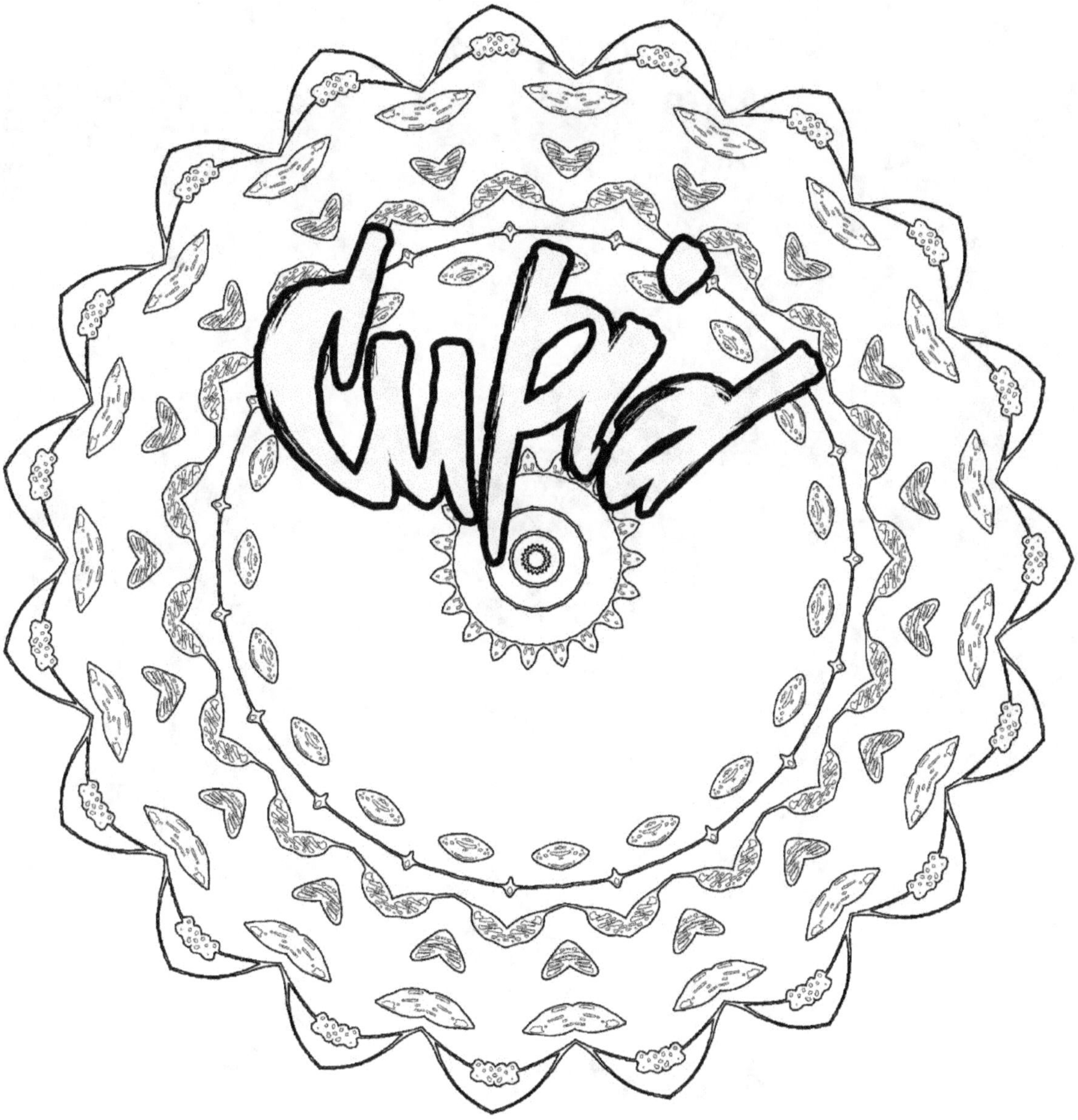

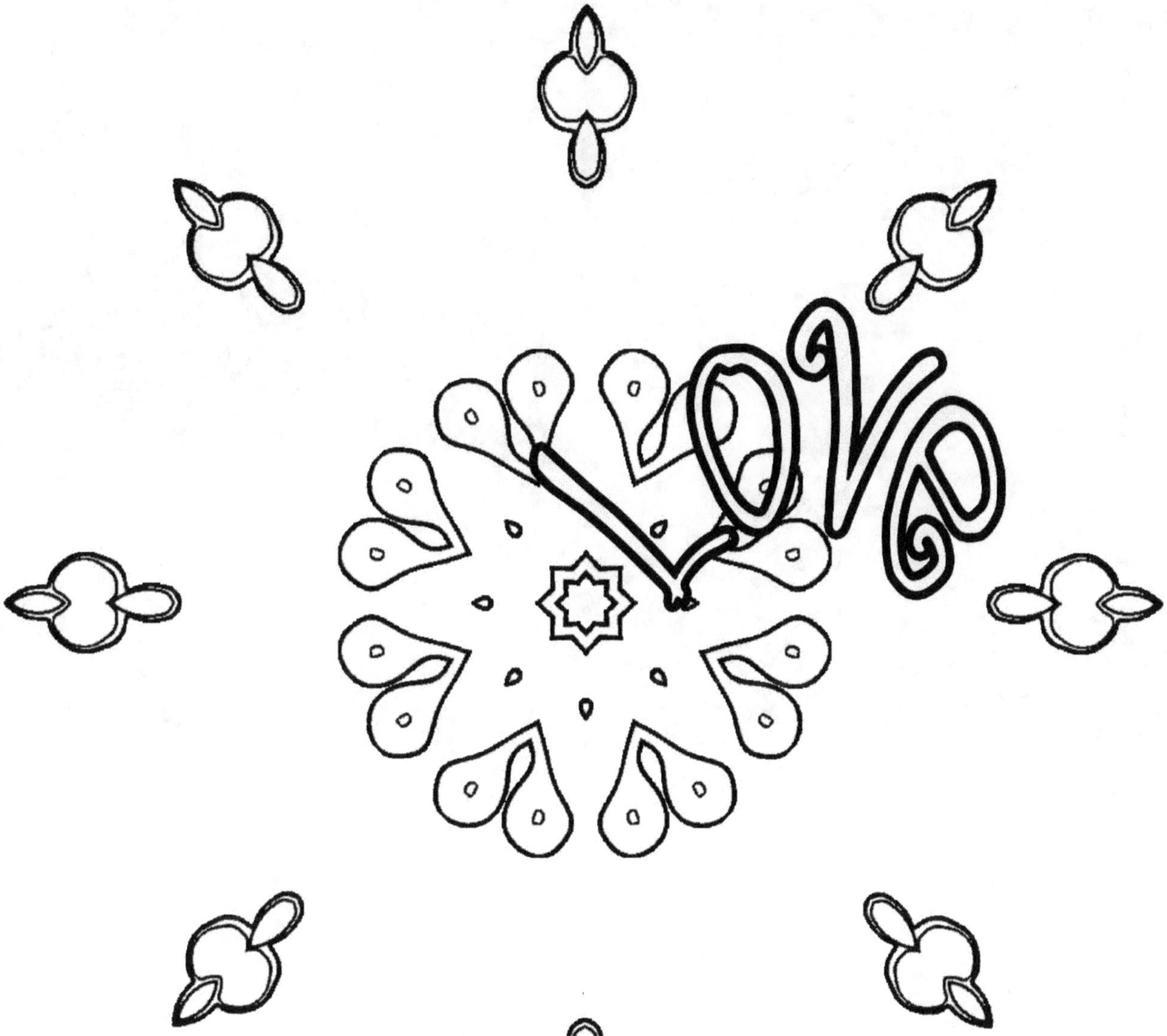
Love

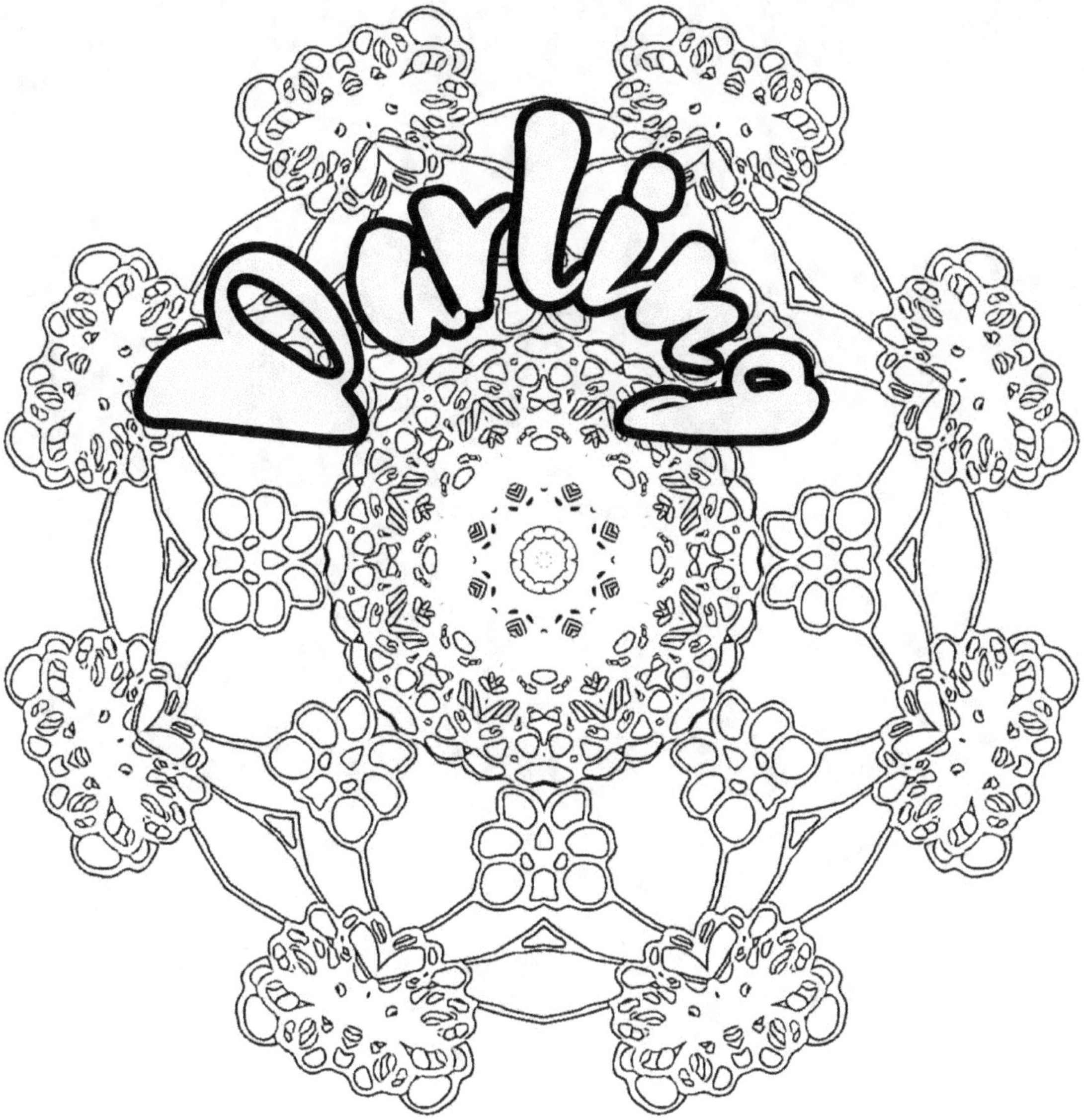
Darling

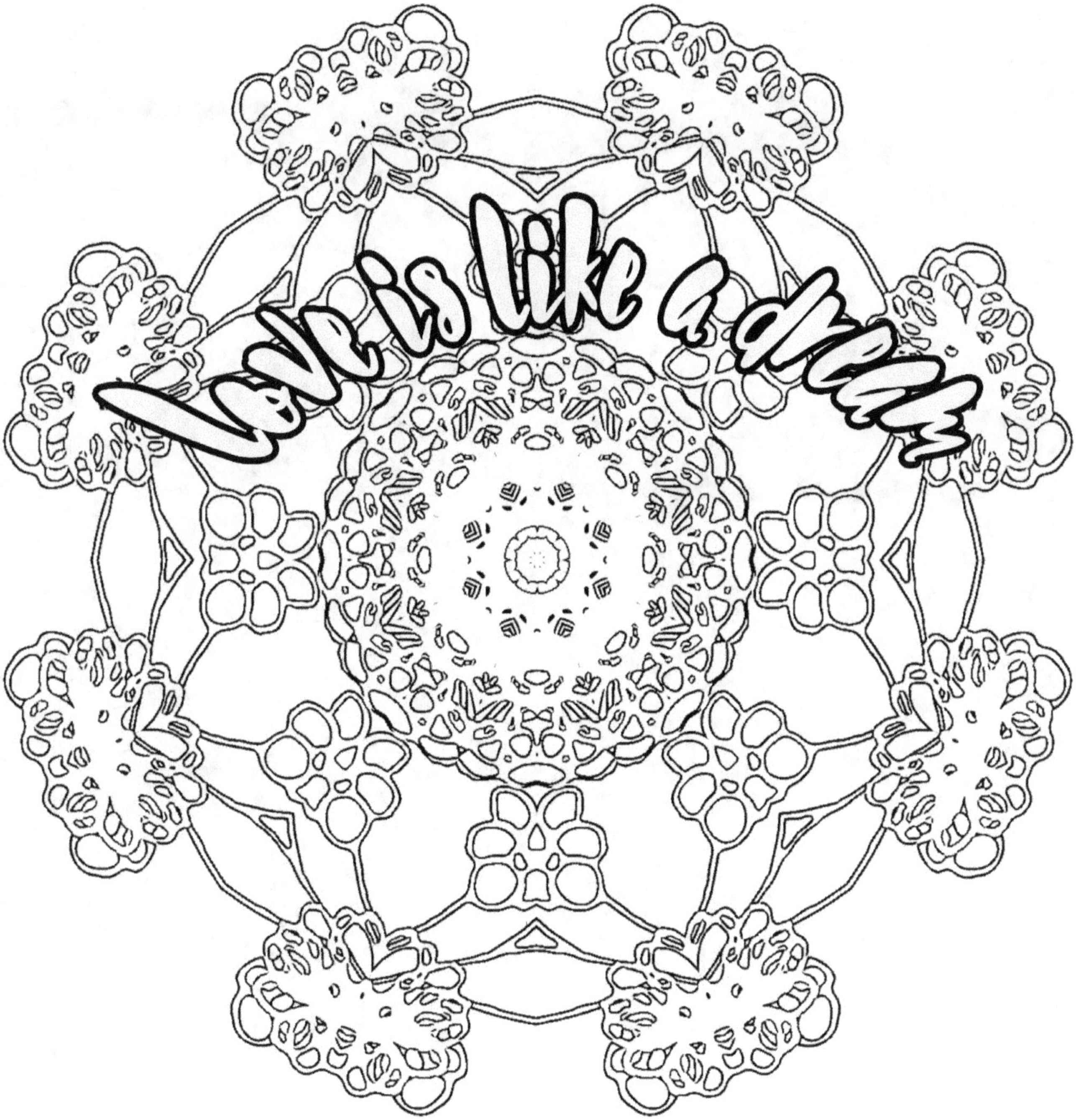
love is like a dream

Love is like a cloud

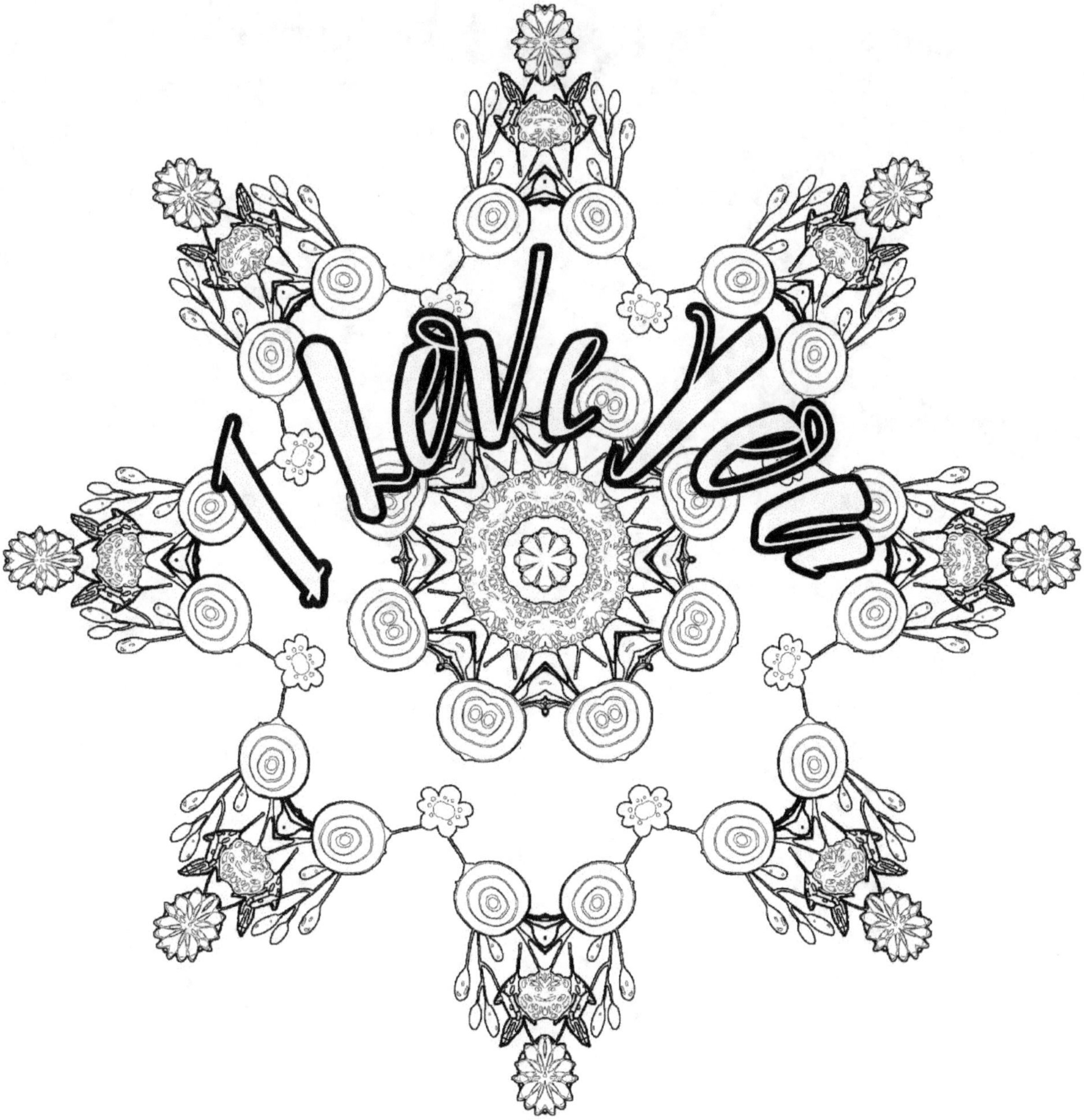
I Love You

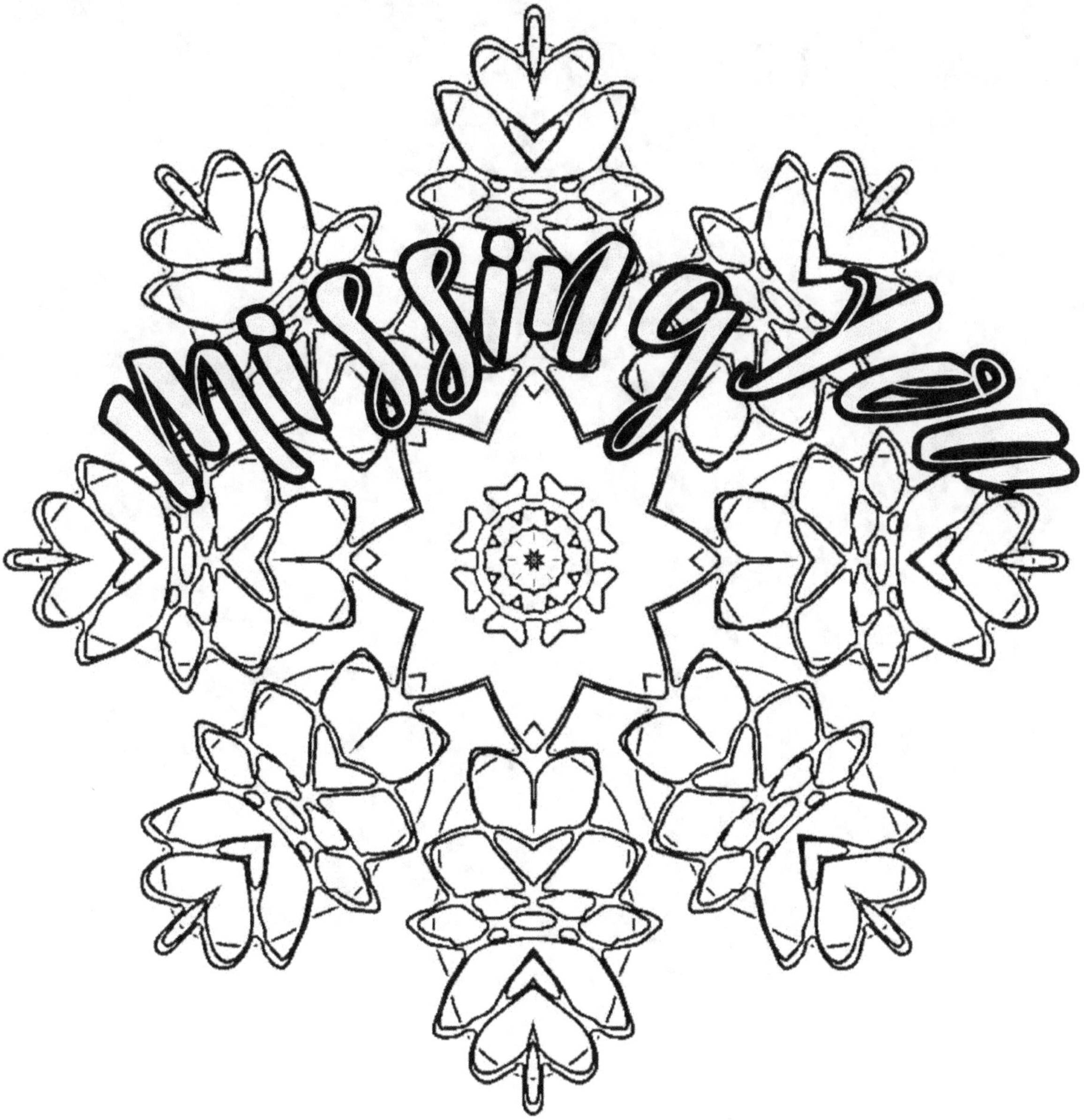
Missing You

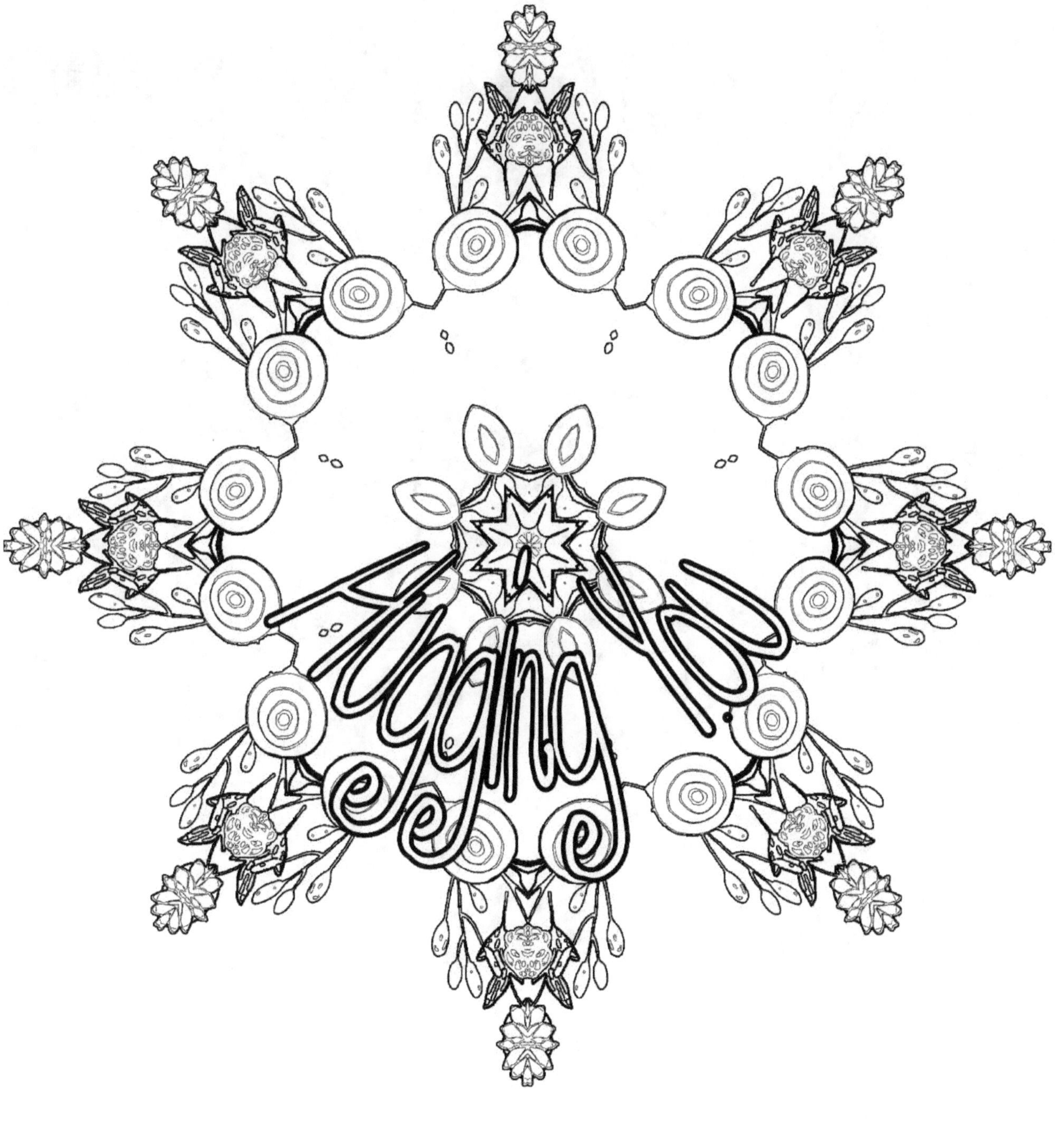
Hugging You

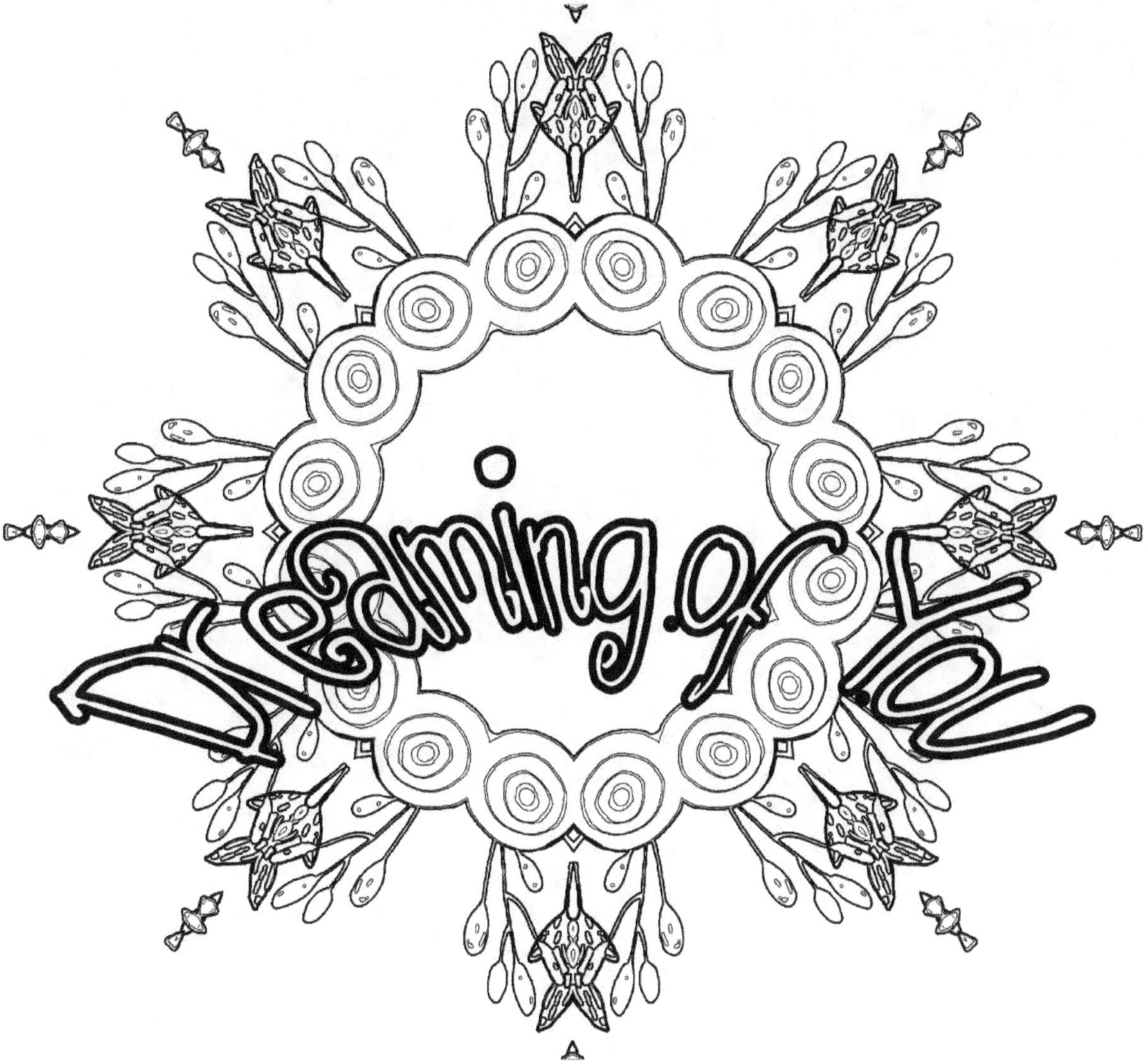
Dreaming of You

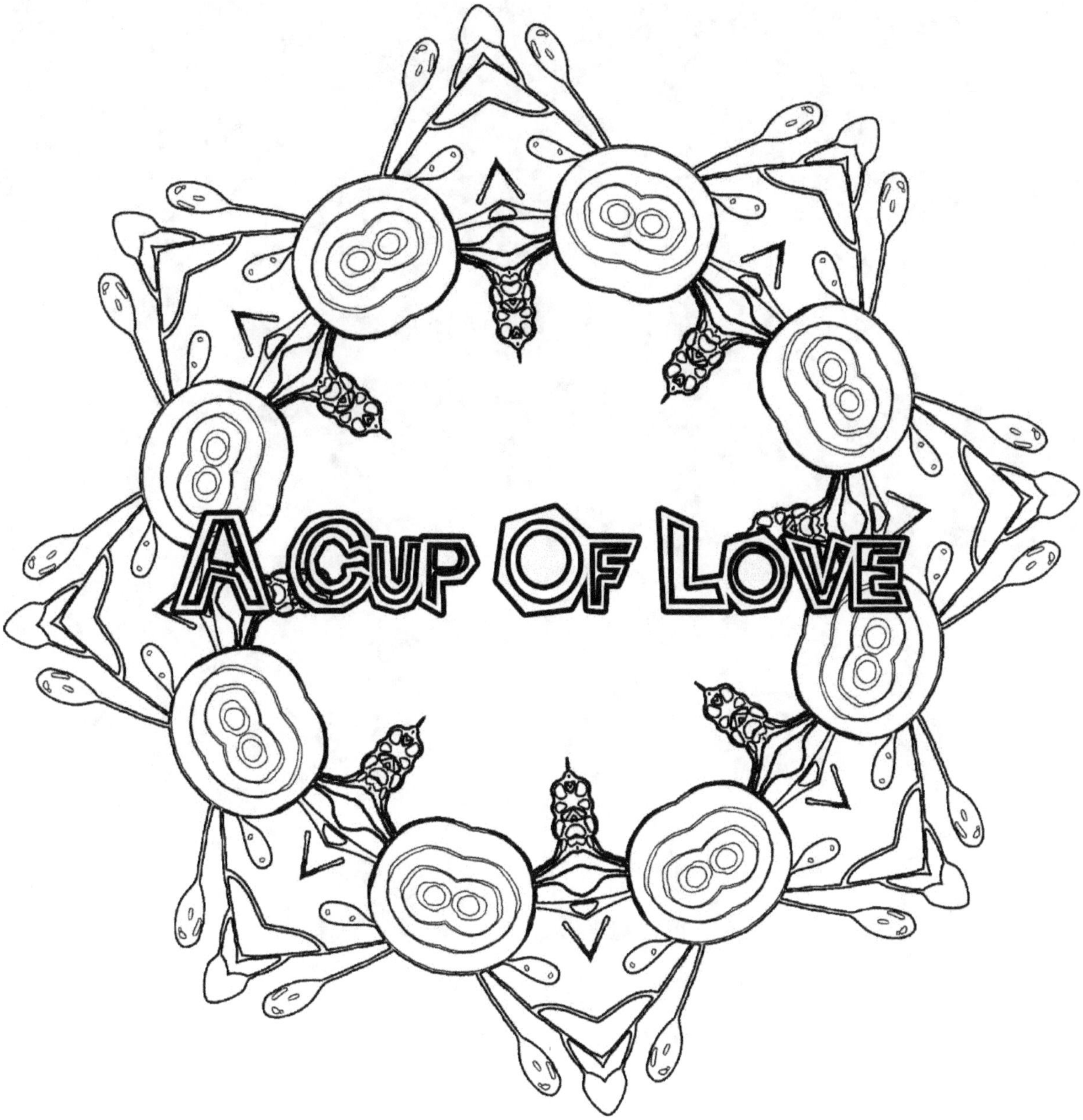
A Cup Of Love

Love in the Mist

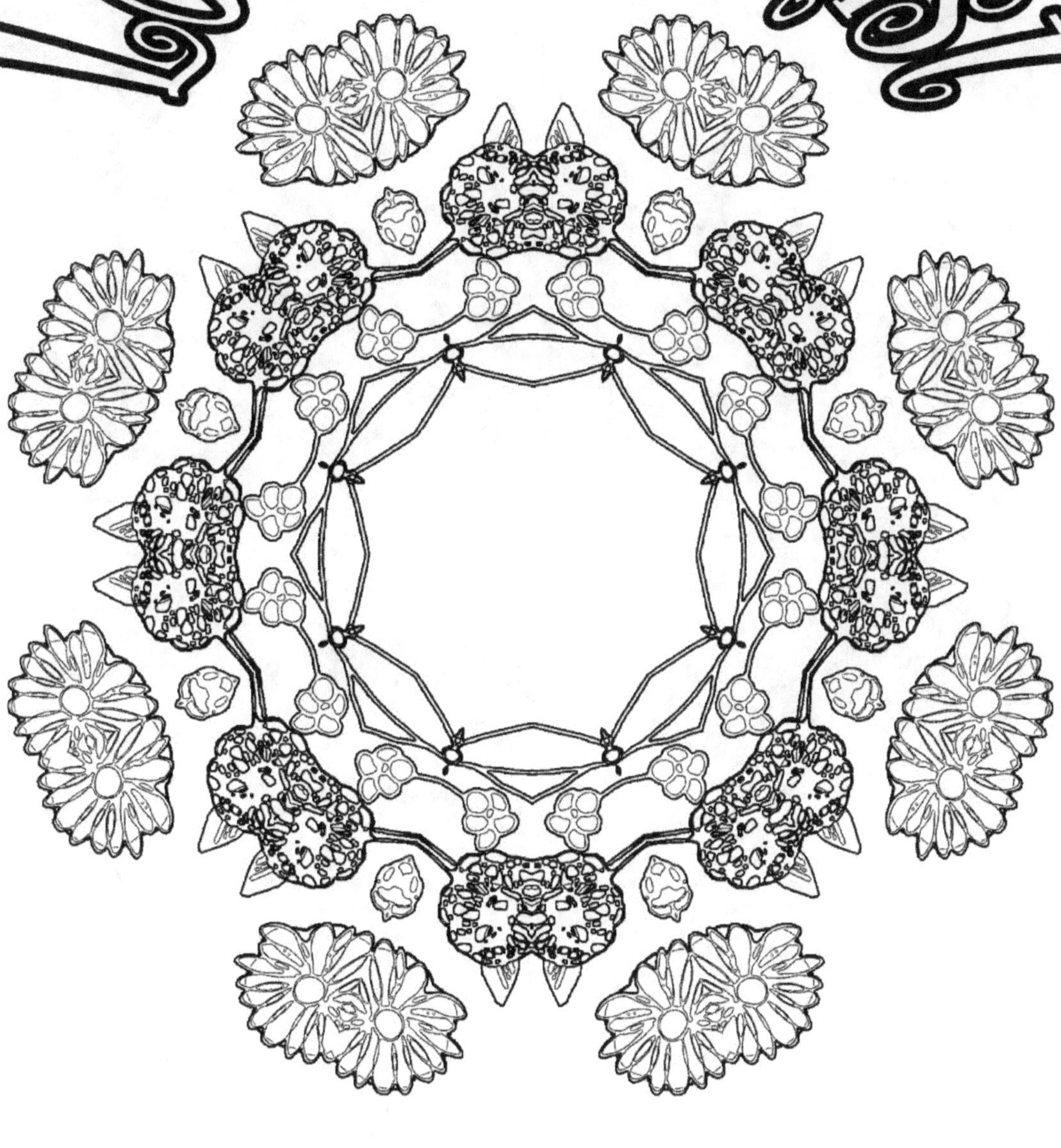

Love at the first site

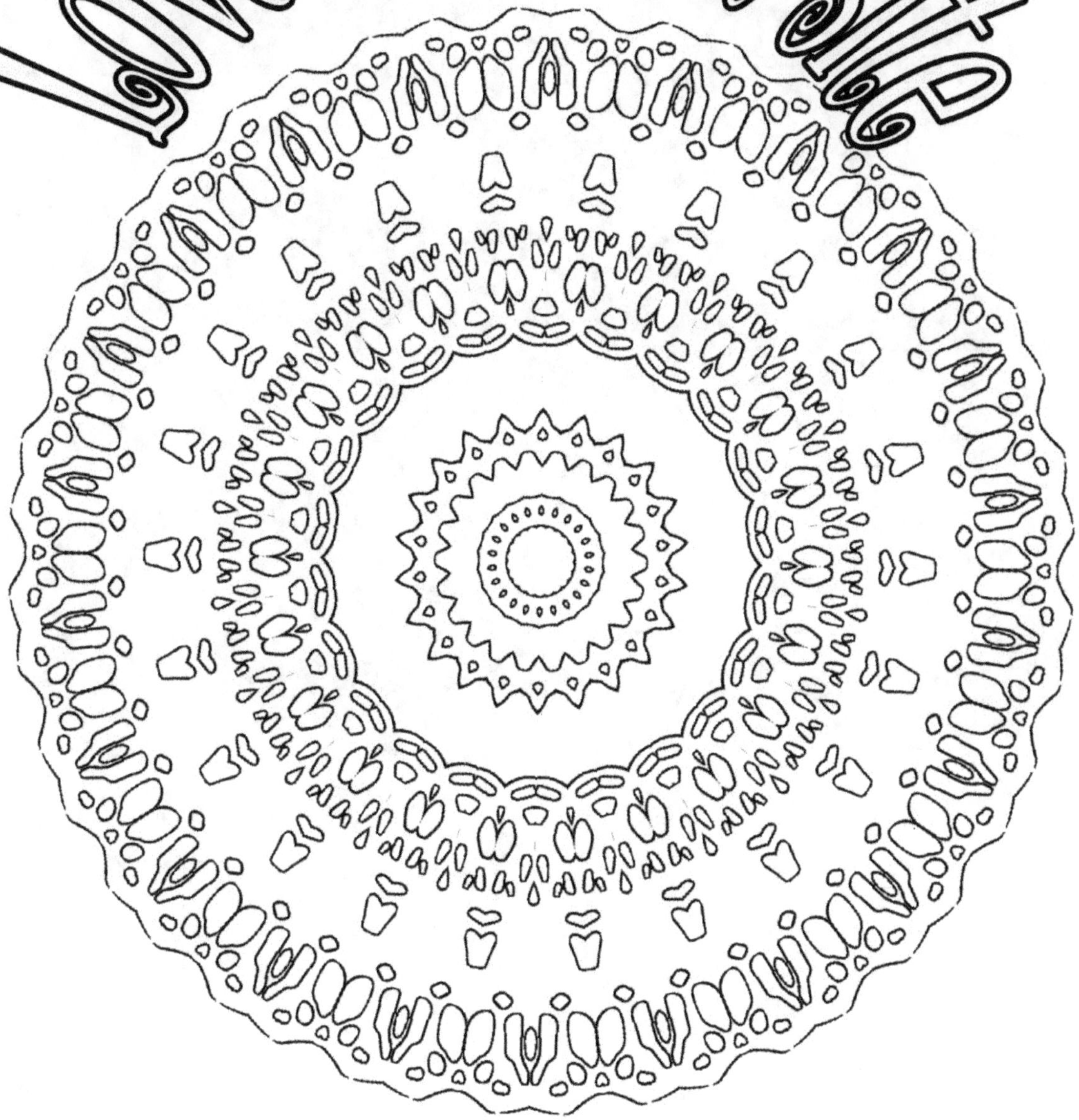

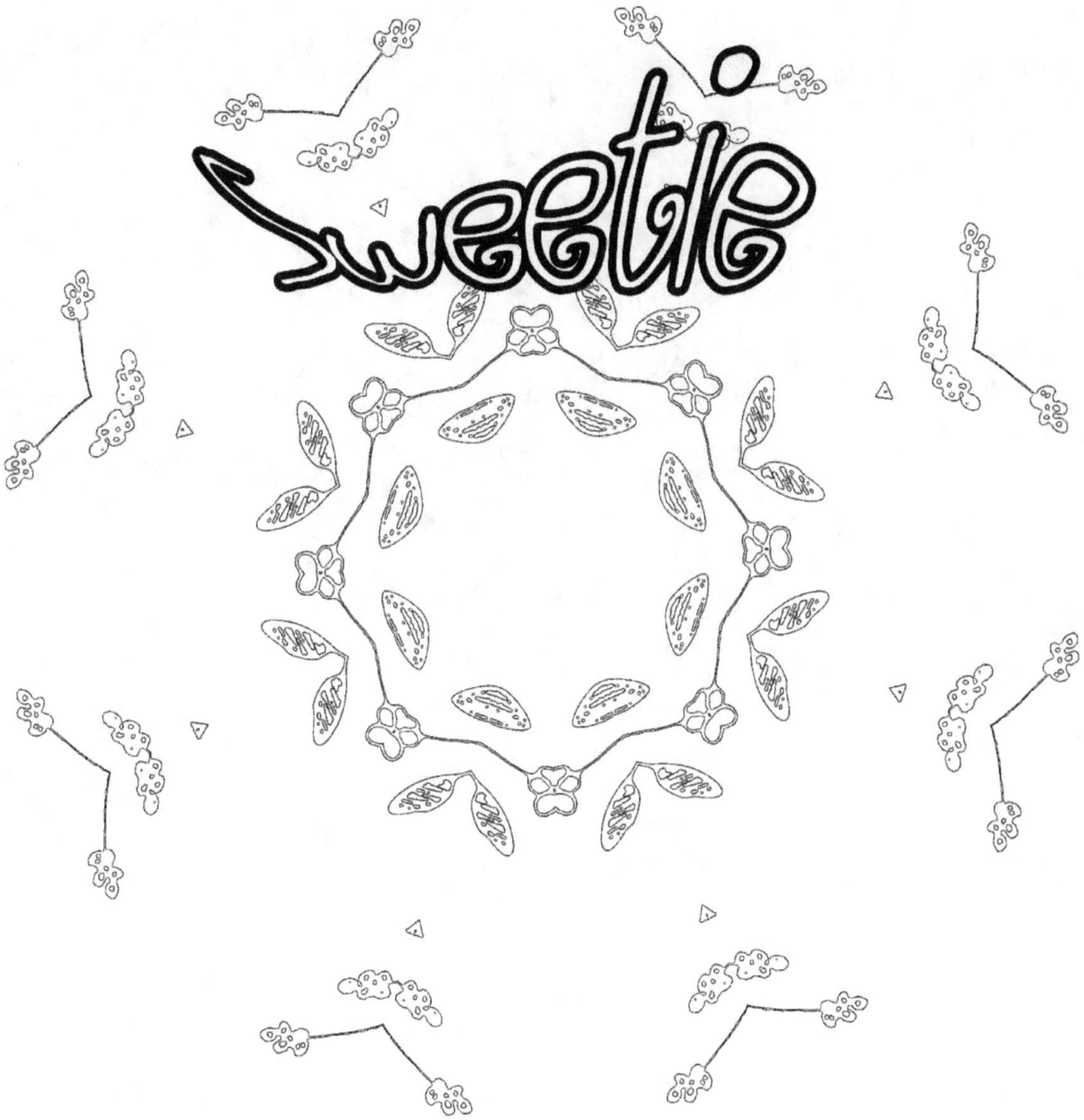
Sweetie

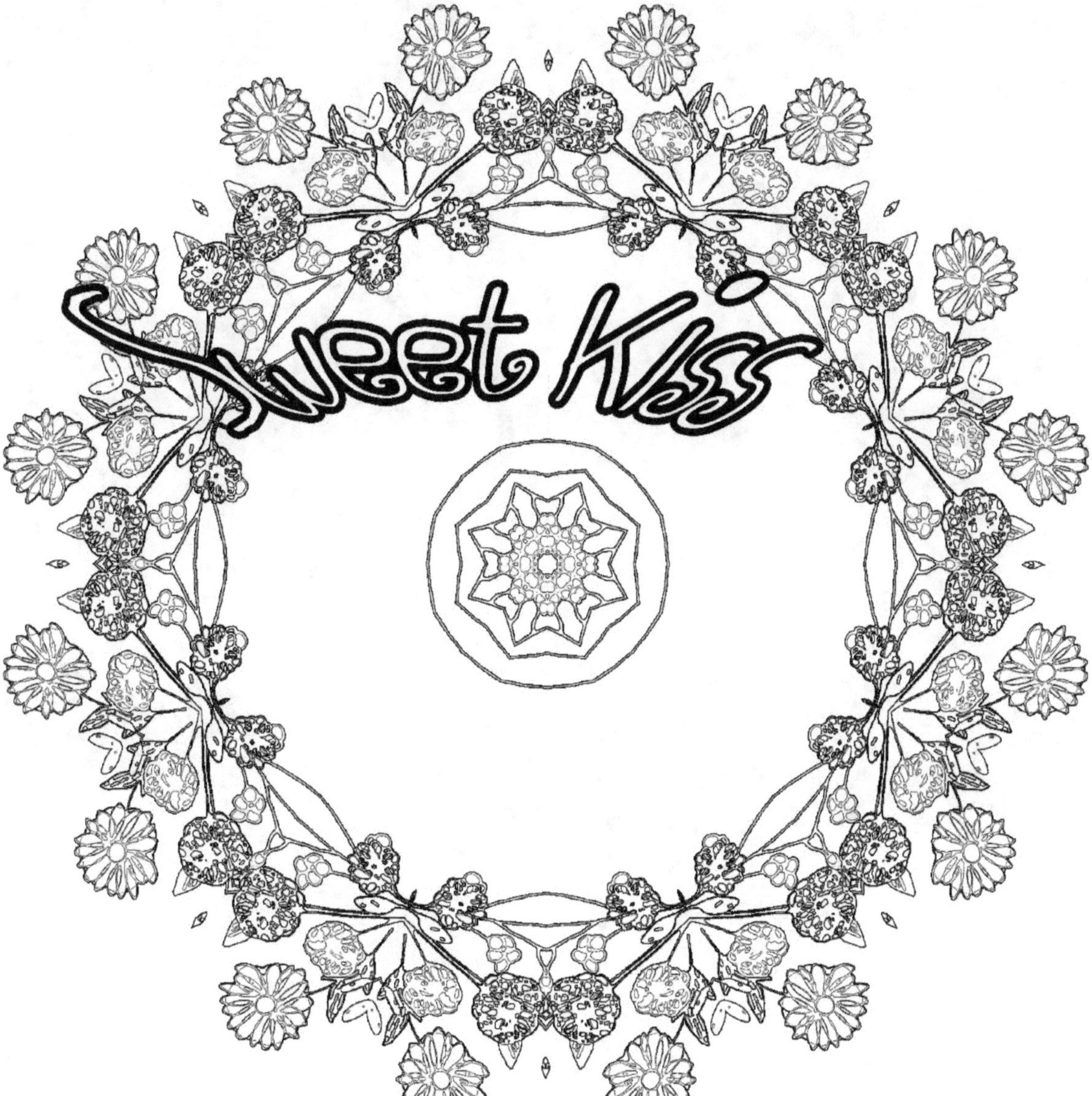
Sweet Kiss

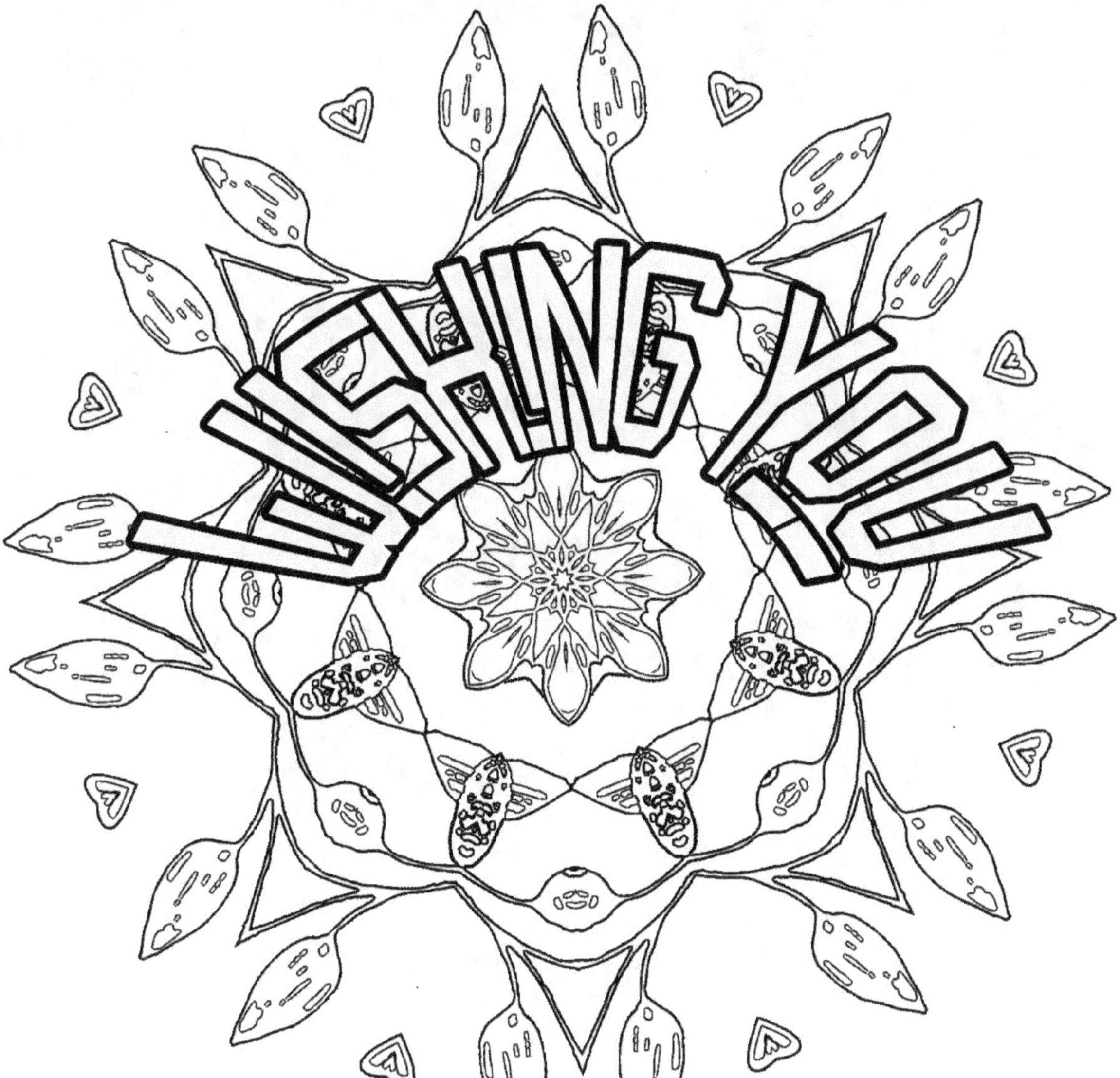
WISHING YOU

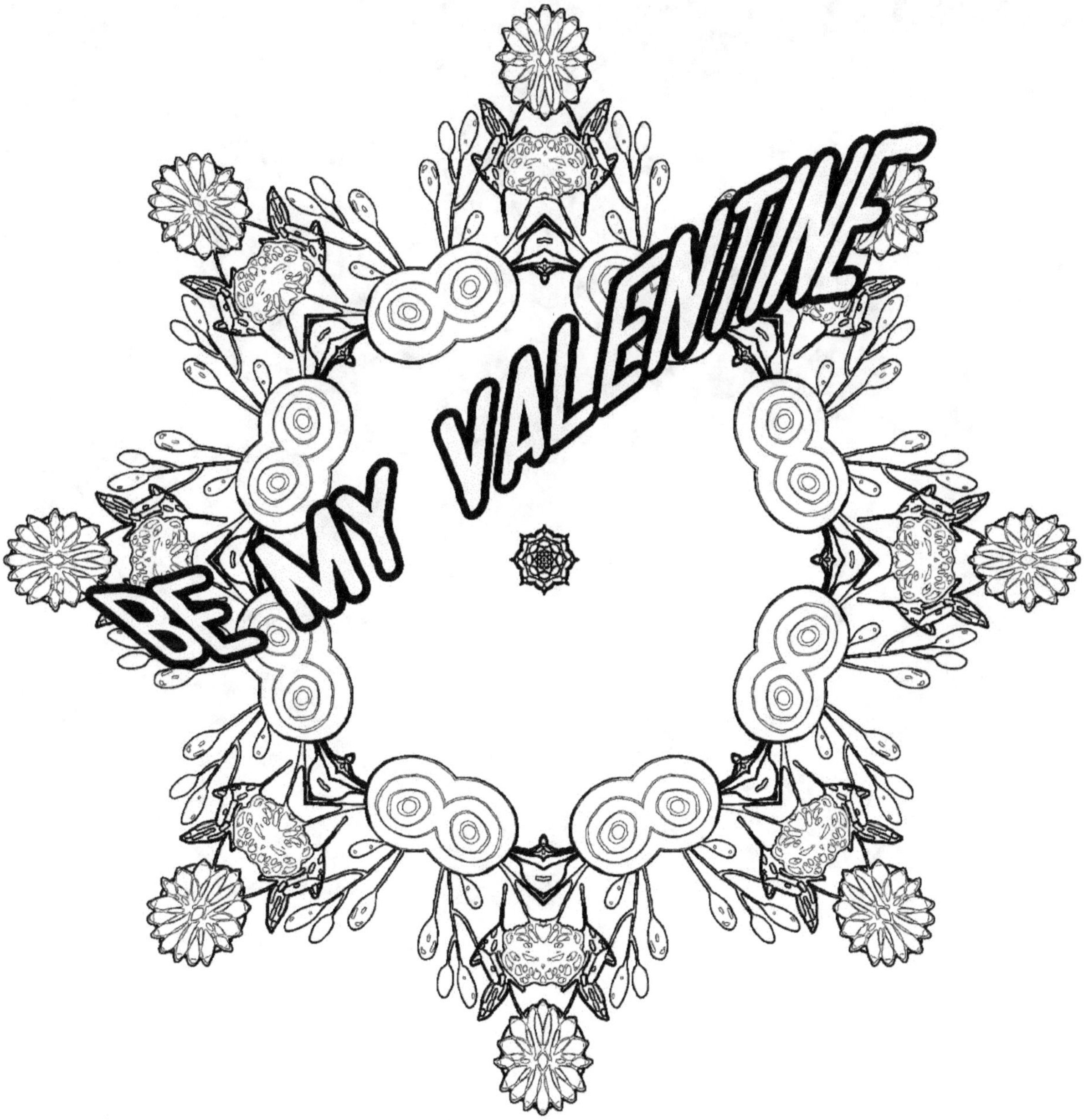
BE MY VALENTINE

www.ingramcontent.com/pod-product-compliance
Lightning Source LLC
Chambersburg PA
CBHW081748170526
45167CB00009B/3966